# The Shocker Book

# The
# Shocker

Two in the Pink
## One in the Stink

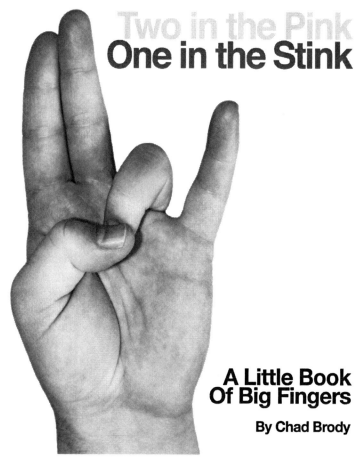

## A Little Book
## Of Big Fingers

### By Chad Brody

**shockerbook.com**
Los Angeles - Las Vegas - Miami - Phoenix - New Jersey

HUMOR / Form / Limericks & Verse
HUMOR / Topic / Adult
HUMOR / General

Published by shockerbook.com

ISBN: 978-0-615-45163-3

First Edition.

# Table of Contents

# Disclaimer

This book contains material that may be considered crude and vulgar. The humor, while immature, might be better left for adults. If you don't like dirty jokes, don't read this book.

You have been warned, so now you can't be *shocked*...

# Preface

The shocker is one of our culture's most enduring urban legends. Known also by its trademark rhyme, "Two in the pink, one in the stink," the shocker has earned its place amongst the classics by a slow and steady rise to cultural ubiquity. The over-the-top innuendo of the shocker has made it perhaps the most famous of all dirty jokes. Not surprisingly, most people are disturbed and offended when they find out what the innocent hand gesture really means.

Often dismissed as crude and immature, the shocker is thusly overlooked for its cultural and historical contributions. For instance, did you know that the shocker is one of the last urban legends to be born out of word-of-mouth sharing? Introduced today, it would likely become a disposable internet meme. Even more intriguing is how the shocker has remained a mystery to the uninitiated for so long: a middle finger won't fly in a family photo, but the shocker can slip by unpunished.

The time has come for a deeper thrust into the mystique of the shocker. The time has come for *The Shocker Book*.

Like the shocker itself, this book is made up of two parts:

## Part 1
A brief but intense, critical discussion of the shocker, which serves as the first, only, and most authoritative work ever produced on the subject.

*(Continues...)*

## Part II

365 variations on the hilarious, "Two in the pink, one in the stink" rhyme; Enough for every day of the year.

You might think about the first part like a textbook, and the second like a joke book. While the first part is a museum, the second is a comedy club. Part I is like two harmless fingers with Part II a wild pinky catching you by surprise.

I'm certain that if you're reading this book it's probably because you not only know what the shocker is, but also because **you get the joke**. And so, this book is for you.

Pinky promise,
Chad Brody

Part 1

# What is the Shocker?

The shocker is a sexually suggestive hand gesture, accompanied by an evocative rhyme, the most popular of which being "Two in the pink, one in the stink." With the index and middle fingers held together and pointed out, the ring finger curled in, and the pinky extended, the shocker implies that the index and middle fingers are to be inserted into a vagina, and the pinky finger into an anus.

The shocker has become an urban legend, and is typically understood to be a dirty joke.

Let's have a look:

**Figure 1A** - *The Shocker*

The shocker can be made with the hand facing either direction, inward or outward, and as we will discuss, the thumb can be tucked in or stuck out as well.

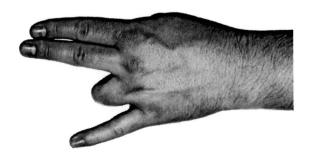

**Figure 1B** - *The Shocker (reverse)*

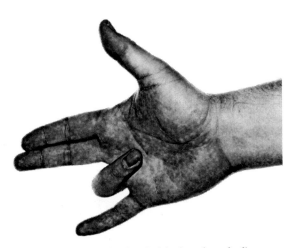

**Figure 1C** - *The Shocker (with thumb cocked)*

It should be noted that the shocker is considered a hand gesture and not a sex move because it is very rarely actually performed on (or *in*, as the case may be...) a woman.

# What's So Funny?

The shocker is funny for two reasons.

First is the innuendo, or what the shocker is referring to. The notion that the shocker would actually be given to a woman is ridiculous(!), and therefore hilarious.

Second, of course, is the rhyme that expresses that innuendo. The lines of a shocker rhyme abstract and analogize a funny sexual surprise into clever and witty word play.

**The hand gesture itself is not funny**. The shocker hand gesture simply *alludes* to what is funny. The performance of the hand gesture also serve to express an endorsement of the crude humor and/or deviant sexual behavior that the rhyme hints at.

Despite any humorous and lighthearted intentions, the shocker is considered to be immature and bordering on vulgar, and has a propensity to offend people when explained. I hope you will agree: **These people probably just have a big pinky up their ass**.

*The Shocker Book*

# "Two in the Pink..."

As we've already learned, the shocker is really half about a hand gesture, half about a rhyme. The most popular shocker rhyme is unquestionably "Two in the Pink, One in the Stink," a version so common it is almost always mentioned when the shocker itself is mentioned. In case you don't get the reference, "Two in the pink" refers to the insertion of the first two fingers of the shocker in woman's vagina, which is generally pink in color, and "One in the stink" refers to the pinky finger going into an anus. Assholes make shit, and shit "stinks." Get it?

The criteria for a shocker rhyme is that the first and last words of each line rhyme; and that the first refers to a vagina, and the second to an anus. Important to understand here is that **the innuendo expressed by those rhymed words is what makes the shocker so funny**. Therefore, the more clever that the words used to refer to vagina and anus are, the funnier the rhyme is, and the funnier the shocker is.

Usually the next in rhyme mentioned after "Two in the pink..." is "Two in the goo, one in the poo." It is not often that it goes beyond this, but there have been situations when a group of people have expanded on the joke and come up with maybe five to ten other versions.

Ever the overachiever, I have written 365 shocker rhymes, which you will read and laugh with in Part II of this book. Some are established classics, but almost all are original. It is a turning point in shocker history. If you think you have come up with a good rhyme yourself, you can submit it at shockerbook.com!

16

# Origin

The origin of the shocker is unknown. Furthermore, its rise to widespread knowledge is also relatively unknown. For these reasons, **the shocker is an archetypal representation of an urban legend**.

We can guess that the shocker came about in the early 1990s. In my research for this book, I found that most Generation Y members had heard of the shocker, with considerable less knowledge amongst Generation X members. Of the Baby Boomers I sampled, none knew the shocker. As internet technology grew in the early 2000s, it allowed photos to be spread and shared faster and easier, and the shocker became much more visible. In addition to movie cameos, numerous comedians have worked the joke into their routines. The gesture has even given rise to an entire economy of products, from stickers to t-shirts, all the way to sex toys.

There has even been a critically acclaimed book published about the shocker.

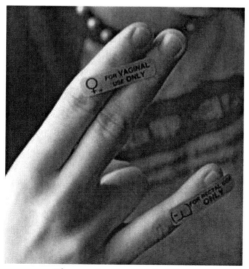

**Figure 4** - *Smell My Fingers*

# Etymology and Usage

The shocker gets its name from the fact that it would be given unbeknownst to the owner of the vagina and anus in question (hereafter, the "shockee"), who is then "shocked" that someone would stick a finger in her ass while manually pleasuring her vagina. It is not unreasonable to assume that in the throes of passion, a woman would be *shocked* when her partner stuck a pinky in her butt hole.

The shocker itself is a noun, whether concrete in defining the hand gesture, or abstract in defining the rhyme and concept of shocking someone. More interestingly, though, are the verbs that accompany the shocker. The shocker can be:

- Given (Like "Giving the finger"),
- Thrown,
- Thrown Up,
- Rocked
- Slipped, and
- Plunged,

...Just to name a few.

## Examples

"Oh my God, bro, did you slip her the shocker!?"

"I threw up the shocker on my way out of the casino, bitches."

"I heard Katie rocked the shocker in her fake ID photo!"

# Thumbs Up

The shocker is popularly expressed with the thumb tucked, holding the ring finger in place. It is also perfectly acceptable to leave the thumb out. In fact, the thumb out and cocked is meant to imply that it is free to stimulate the clitoris of the vagina that the index and middle fingers are plunging.

As such, when a shocker is displayed with the thumb out, the thumb is usually wiggled, implying it is stimulating the clitoris.

**Figure 6** - *Thumb Stimulation*

# Shock and Awe

The shocker is loved and loathed. In preparing this book, I conducted a great deal of research, some of which by holding interviews about the shocker with random people.

Common responses by people for whom the shocker tends to be seen as immature included groans and condescending eye rolls. However, despite an unfavorable opinion, they did possess rudimentary knowledge about the shocker. A popular opinion I found amongst this camp is that someone who is versed with the shocker must be a "bro" or a "douche-bag" who revels in misogynist humor, though the humor behind the shocker is not technically misogynist. "Shocker-haters" generally looked down on anyone who might throw up a shocker in a photo.

However, in other interviews, great bonds were forged over talk of the shocker, with many people having stories to tell about their own experiences with the shocker, always as a joke. Interestingly, nobody I interviewed has ever been given or tried to give the shocker; everyone who thought the shocker was funny understood the joke. Most responses were positive. In fact, what I found is that the shocker has a very large following.

A lot the positive reactions generally came from adolescents (Both male and female). Perhaps the shocker is an apt symbol for adolescence, as it reflects the knowledge of sex and sexual acts, but still treats them as humorous. "Haha, that's gross!" was a common response, probably because for kids that age, gross stuff is funny.

There is much evidence that supports that the shocker is not merely for kids. For instance, the shocker has spawned an entire merchandise economy. Products as diverse as sticker, t-shirts, hats, gloves (with pink and brown fingers), and sex toys have all been created in its likeness. (All of the aforementioned and more are available for purchase at shockerbook.com, so make sure to check it out).

There are countless websites and social media pages that exist for the shocker, too.

What I found in my research points at the obvious: The shocker is undoubtedly part of our collective unconscious, whether we like it or are completely appalled by it.

**Figure 7** - *Shocker Merchandise*

# Say Cheese
# (And Throw Up a Shocker)

The shocker is most often given in photographs. In fact, throwing up a shocker while someone is taking your picture has probably been the single most popular way of propagating and perpetuating the shocker's mythology. The shocker can provide comic relief in an otherwise serious photo. A picture of you with a shocker hand juxtaposed against the backdrop of the Grand Canyon or a geyser takes an otherwise boring tourist photo and adds a little light-hearted fun. When a fraternity takes a group photo, it is often customary for all of the members to give the shocker, mirroring their brotherhood of fraternity with the brotherhood of the shocker.

**Figure 8** - *Stick Out Those Pinkies, Ladies...*

Much like young Japanese girls always put up a V sign in photographs, so do many young people in America put up a shocker. The more serious the photo, the more fun it is to rock the shocker!

Since the shocker can't offend you if you don't know what it is, it's generally a safe way to show one's initiation into the knowledge of the shocker. In this capacity, it works just like a gang sign: If you know, you know. If you don't, fuck you.

# Variations

The following are a small collection of hand gestures that aren't anywhere near as popular as the shocker, except for the rocker of course, but it is not popular in this context. They are sometimes demonstrated once someone has broken the shocker ice, and so shall be included in our discussion. It is implied by the photos that the top half of the fingers are for vaginal stimulation, and the bottom for anal.

**Figure 9A** - *The Teaser*

**Figure 9B** - *The Pleaser*

*(Continues...)*

**Figure 9C** - *The Rocker*

**Figure 9D** - *The Spocker*

**Figure 9E** - *Das Showstopper*

# No Means No

As we've come to learn, the shocker is generally harmless, as only the people who know about it are the ones sharing it; those who are offended just aren't going to go throw up the shocker in a photo. Again, the logic is that if you don't know what it means, you can't be offended. However, if you do know what it means, you can be offended.

One example takes place in 2009, when a shocker app was developed for the iPhone. It was rejected by Apple and therefore not released into the iTunes App Store. A man named Richard, who also rejected the Google Voice app, is responsible for the rejection of the Shocker App. [*Editor's Note: The initial rejection of the Google Voice app is considered by many to be the major turning point in Google-Apple relations, which ultimately became very bitter.* ]

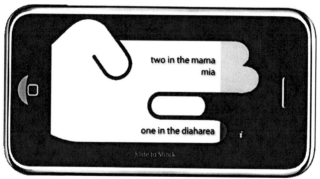

**Figure 10** - *The Shocker for iPhone*

Richard's primary reasoning was, "What if a child saw this?" The developers pled their case to Richard and to his boss: "So what if a kid saw, would the kid know what it meant? Would a parent have to explain? Would the parent even know!?" Despite this, and despite worse apps in the app store, there will be no Shocker App for iOS. Why? Simple: **Richard knew what the shocker was, and he was offended.**

# Stumped

Here's a submission of a real-life shocker, in which the ring finger is a stump. Awesome! Theoretically, this man can **go deep** when giving the shocker.

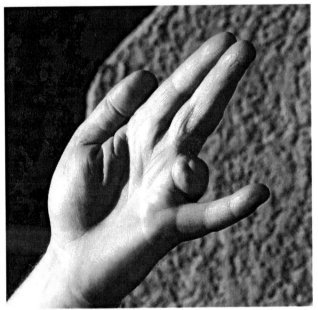

**Figure 11** - *Doesn't wear a ring, but he is married...*

Now let's get to the jokes!

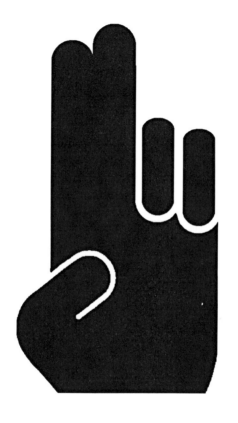

Part II

# 365 Shocker Rhymes

The following is the world's largest compilation of shocker rhyme/jokes in history. I originally wrote these 365 rhymes for a daily desk calendar, and now they are available to you in book form, like a collection of haiku or classic verse. They are randomly sorted. Some will resonate with you better than others, but I hope they all bring you the smile the shocker is known for.

If you think I've missed one, please don't hesitate to submit it at shockerbook.com!

Enjoy!

Two in the Needy,
One in the Bleedy.


Two in the Virgin,
One in the Purgin'.


Two in the Slug,
One in the Plug.

Two in the Boat,
One in the Goat.

Two in the Tool,
One in the Mule.

Two in the Close,
One in the Gross.

Two in the Clit,
One in the Shit.

Two in the Willy,
One in the Chili.

Two in the Lips,
One in the Hips.

Two in the Muff,
One in the Buff.

Two in the Slush,
One in the Flush.

Two in the Squeek,
One in the Greek.

Two in the Chute,
One in the Poot.

Two in the Moist,
One in the Choice.

Two in the Pee,
One in the Big D.

Two in the Clincher,
One in the Pincher.

Two in the Lips,
One in the Chips.

Two in the Stain,
One in the Ain.

Two in the Womb,
One in the Tomb.


Two in the Baby,
One in the Maybe.


Two in the Tide,
One in the Bride.


Two in the Pain,
One in the Ain.


Two in the Heinous,
One in the Anus.

Two in the Kitten,
One in the Sittin'.


Two in the Cutie,
One in the Pooty.


Two in the Snatch,
One in the Dingleberry Patch.


Two in the Catcher's Mitt,
One in the Shit.


Two in the Lass,
One in the Ass.

Two in the Mush,
One in the Flush.

Two in the Shave,
One in the Cave.

Two in the Blossom,
One in the Awesome.

Two in the Nut,
One in the Butt.

Two in the Slime,
One in the Grime.

Two in the Hype,
One in the Ripe.


Two in the Shag,
One in the Stag.


Two in the Honey,
One in the Money.


Two in the Tide,
One in the Slide.


Two in the Fertile,
One in the Turtle.

Two in the Mutt,
One in the Butt.

Two in the Goo,
One in the Poo.

Two in the Blowed,
One in the Load.

Two in the Jowels,
One in the Bowels.

Two in the Meat,
One in the Seat.

Two in the Poon,
One in the Moon.


Two in the Toy,
One in the Boy.


Two in the Spread,
One in the Shed.


Two in the Twat,
One in the Squat.


Two in the Girl,
One in the Swirl.

Two in the Cuddle,
One in the Mud Puddle.

Two in the Gash,
One in the Cash.

Two in the Crabs,
One in the Scabs.

Two in the Future,
One in the Suture.

Two in the City,
One in the Shitty.

Two in the Inches,
One in the Pinches.

Two in the Gusher,
One in the Flusher.

Two in the Munge,
One in the Plunge.

Two in the Shoot,
One in the Toot.

Two in the Pork,
One in the Cork.

Two in the Chit Chat,
One in the Hit That.


Two in the Hammer,
One in the Slammer.


Two in the Poop,
One in the Goop.


Two in the Jewels,
One in the Rules!


Two in the Child,
One in the Wild.

Two in the Knoll,
One in the Hole.

Two in the Preggo,
One in the Leggo.

Two in the Flirt,
One in the Hurt.

Two in the Eat,
One in the Seat.

Two in the Yoni,
One in the Chonie.

Two in the Cooty,
One in the Booty.

Two in the Jam,
One in the Ham.

Two in the Cock,
One in the Shock.

Two in the Stain,
One in the Pain.

Two in the Snail,
One in the Tail.

Two in the Squirt,
One in the Hurt.

Two in the Mother,
One in the Brother.

Two in the Sticky,
One in the Icky.

Two in the Funs,
One in the Runs.

Two in the Crack,
One in the Back.

Two in the Clap,
One in the Trap.

Two in the Muff,
One in the Rough.

Two in the Rag,
One in the Fag.

Two in the Mother,
One in the Other.

Two in the Church,
One in the Lurch.

Two in the Happy,
One in the Crappy.

Two in the Pipe,
One in the Wipe.

Two in the Sister,
One in the Fister.

Two in the Skunk,
One in the Funk.

Two in the Twist,
One in the Fist.

Two in the Vag,
One in the Badge.

Two in the Valley,
One in the Alley.

Two in the Snug,
One in the Plug.

Two in the Pee,
One in the Potourri.

Two in the Classy,
One in the Gassy.

Two in the Snowball,
One in the 911 Call.


Two in the Sass,
One in the Ass.


Two in the Chop,
One in the Plop.


Two in the In,
One in the Sin.


Two in the Fupa,
One in the Poopa.

Two in the Ride,
One in the Hide.

Two in the Bush,
One in the Moosh.

Two in the Cooter,
One in the Shooter.

Two in the Fuck,
One in the Chuck.

Two in the Giney,
One in the Hiney.

Two in the Bald,
One in the Maulled.

Two in the Douche,
One in the Touche.

Two in the Chatter,
One in the Splatter.

Two in the Shoot,
One in the Shute.

Two in the Gap,
One in the Crap.

Two in the Hot,
One in the Squat.

Two in the Chewey,
One in the Pooey.

Two in the Snaggle,
One in the Waggle.

Two in the Chug,
One in the Plug.

Two in the Gutter,
One in the Cutter.

Two in the Flirt,
One in the Dirt.


Two in the Mild,
One in the Wild.


Two in the Lass,
One in the Gas.


Two in the Pimp,
One in the Gimp.


Two in the Dame,
One in the Shame.

Two in the Mum,
One in the Bum.

Two in the Double,
One in the Trouble.

Two in the Snake,
One in the Break.

Two in the Ballad,
One in the Salad.

Two in the Weak,
One in the Freak.

Two in the Cutie,
One in the Booty.

Two in the Pocket,
One in the Chocolate.

Two in the Happy,
One in the Nappy.

Two in the Poker,
One in the Choker.

Two in the Sludge,
One in the Fudge.

Two in the Grass,
One in the Ass.

Two in the Hitter,
One in the Shitter.

Two in the Boss,
One in the Floss.

Two in the Chat,
One in the Splat.

Two in the Cunt ,
One in the Grunt.

Two in the Rain,
One in the Stain.


Two in the Tasted,
One in the Wasted.


Two in the Party,
One in the Farty.


Two in the Pink Slot,
One in the Stink Pot.


Two in the Right,
One in the Tight.

Two in the Cockswain,
One in the Pain.

Two in the Down,
One in the Brown.

Two in the Wonder,
One in the Blunder.

Two in the Crisco,
One in the Frisco.

Two in the Eve,
One in the Cleave.

Two in the Stoop,
One in the Poop.

Two in the Choach,
One in the Roach.

Two in the Fuck,
One in the Yuck.

Two in the Pie,
One in the Eye.

Two in the Gash,
One in the Stash.

Two in the Nad,
One in the Dad.

Two in the Pleasure,
One in the Treasure.

Two in the Box,
One in the Rocks.

Two in the Queef,
One in the Beef.

Two in the Cancer,
One in the Answer.

Two in the Clown,
One in the Brown.

Two in the Fun,
One in the Bun.

Two in the Rape,
One in the Gape.

Two in the Bloody,
One in the Muddy.

Two in the Loose,
One in the Mouse.

Two in the Red,
One in the Dead.

Two in the Slit,
One in the Mitt.

Two in the Curtain,
One in the Hurtin'.

Two in the Gear,
One in the Rear.

Two in the Slop,
One in the Plop.

Two in the Lick,
One in the Sick.

Two in the Musk,
One in the Husk.

Two in the Glad,
One in the Sad.

Two in the Trout,
One in the Out.

Two in the Beard,
One in the Weird.

Two in the Nag,
One in the Gag.

Two in the Ripe,
One in the Wipe.

Two in the Blood,
One in the Mud.

Two in the Moss,
One in the Toss.

Two in the Funs,
One in the Buns.

Two in the Whack,
One in the Crack.

Two in the Clots,
One in the Trots.

Two in the Mound,
One in the Pound.

Two in the Bitch,
One in the Ditch.

Two in the Drip,
One in the Rip.

Two in the Cancer,
One in the Dancer.


Two in the Christ,
One in the Spiced.


Two in the Loose,
One in the Deuce.


Two in the Main,
One in the Pain.


Two in the Musky,
One in the Husky.

Two in the Sock,
One in the Shock.

Two in the Tart,
One in the Fart.

Two in the Jobber,
One in the Slobber.

Two in the Slop Hole,
One in the Plop Hole.

Two in the Kitty,
One in the Shitty.

Two in the Slut,
One in the Butt.

Two in the Play,
One in the Gay.

Two in the Red wings,
One in the It Stings!

Two in the Clam,
One in the Damn!

Two in the Dress,
One in the Mess.

Two in the Hit,
One in the Shit.

Two in the Use,
One in the Abuse.

Two in the Bank,
One in the Stank.

Two in the Gush,
One in the Mush.

Two in the Hump,
One in the Dump.

Two in the Flirty,
One in the Dirty.

Two in the Beave,
One in the Sleave.

Two in the Sauce,
One in the Toss.

Two in the Hit,
One in the Quit.

Two in the Jelly,
One in the Smelly.

Two in the Rug,
One in the Plug.


Two in the Virgin Mary,
One in the Dingleberry.


Two in the Easy,
One in the Sleazy.


Two in the Pump,
One in the Rump.


Two in the Slimey,
One in the Grimey.

Two in the Screamer,
One in the Steamer.

Two in the Twat,
One in the Knot.

Two in the Fold,
One in the Gold.

Two in the Virgin,
One in the Splurgin'.

Two in the Needy,
One in the Seedy.

Two in the Pee,
One in the Spree.

Two in the Clit,
One in the Pit.

Two in the Wet,
One in the Regret.

Two in the Front,
One in the Bunt.

Two in the I have needs,
One in the Anal beads.

Two in the Punanny,
One in the Fanny.

Two in the Scent,
One in the Vent.

Two in the Box,
One in the Knox.

Two in the Glide,
One in the Joyride.

Two in the Pregger,
One in the Beggar.

Two in the Tuna,
One in the luna.

Two in the Coos,
One in the Juice.

Two in the Club,
One in the Tub.

Two in the Man Eater,
One in the Ham Heater.

Two in the Slit,
One in the Shit.

Two in the Ripe,
One in the Pipe.


Two in the Shooter,
One in the Tooter.


Two in the Inches,
One in the Flinches.


Two in the Town,
One in the Brown.


Two in the Town,
One in the Down.

Two in the Freak,
One in the Greek.


Two in the Spunk,
One in the Chunks.


Two in the Bismark,
One in the Tanbark.


Two in the Complain,
One in the Restrain.


Two in the Cute,
One in the Shute.

Two in the Funnel,
One in the Pummel.

Two in the Jane,
One in the Pain.

Two in the Pink,
One in the Stink.

Two in the Humper,
One in the Dumper.

Two in the Slit,
One in the Pit.

Two in the Yes,
One in the Mess.


Two in the Double,
One in the Trouble.


Two in the Poose,
One in the Deuce.


Two in the Hair Pie,
One in the Brown Eye.


Two in the PlayTex,
One in the Latex.

Two in the Doll,
One in the Maul.

Two in the Class,
One in the Gas.

Two in the Fame,
One in the Shame.

Two in the Bald,
One in the Appalled.

Two in the Hag,
One in the Fag.

Two in the Snatch,
One in the Scratch.

Two in the Waffle,
One in the Awful.

Two in the Rumpelstiltskin,
One in the Blumblestiltskin.

Two in the Junk,
One in the Trunk.

Two in the Bone,
One in the Moan.

Two in the Pimping,
One in the Limping.

Two in the Flower,
One in the Sour.

Two in the Scream,
One in the Steam.

Two in the Fucker,
One in the Pucker.

Two in the Gunk,
One in the Funk.

Two in the Headache,
One in the Mistake.


Two in the Ring,
One in the Sting.


Two in the Itch,
One in the Your Bitch.


Two in the Jane,
One in the Insane.


Two in the Snail,
One in the Jail.

Two in the Cunt,
One in the Runt.

Two in the Greet,
One in the Meat.

Two in the Tract,
One in the Jacked.

Two in the Mama Mia,
One in the Diarrhea.

Two in the Fox,
One in the Ox.

Two in the Porn,
One in the Torn.

Two in the Vibe,
One in the Bribe.

Two in the Pouts,
One in the Doubts.

Two in the Pouch,
One in the Grouch.

Two in the Bore,
One in the Whore.

Two in the Erection,
One in the Infection.

Two in the Itches,
One in the Stitches.

Two in the Piss,
One in the Bliss.

Two in the Flap,
One in the Crap.

Two in the Gore,
One in the Sore.

Two in the Pink,
One in the Wink.

Two in the Pipe,
One in the Ripe.

Two in the Cherry,
One in the Scary.

Two in the Hinge,
One in the Cringe.

Two in the Marry,
One in the Bury.

Two in the Tunafish,
One in the Starfish.

Two in the Cherry,
One in the Fairy.

Two in the Hair,
One in the Dare.

Two in the Muff,
One in the Stuff.

Two in the Loose,
One in the Caboose.

Two in the Beaver,
One in the Leave her.


Two in the Beaver,
One in the Fever.


Two in the Stabbin',
One in the Cabin.


Two in the Kitchen,
One in the Bitchin'.


Two in the Clam,
One in the Ham.

Two in the Steam,
One in the Cream.


Two in the Jack,
One in the Crack.


Two in the Slut,
One in the Cut.


Two in the Snag,
One in the Fag.


Two in the Snake,
One in the Shake.

Two in the Taco,
One in the Paco.

Two in the Jingle,
One in the Dingle.

Two in the Mist,
One in the Fist.

Two in the Core,
One in the Tore.

Two in the Furry,
One in the Worry.

Two in the Job,
One in the Slob.

Two in the Willy,
One in the Really!?.

Two in the Chick,
One in the Sick.

Two in the Porn,
One in the Corn.

Two in the Sperm,
One in the Germ.

Two in the Pimp,
One in the Limp.

Two in the Wench,
One in the Stench.

Two in the Door,
One in the Gore.

Two in the Droop,
One in the Poop.

Two in the Heat,
One in the Meat.

Two in the Fish,
One in the Squish.

Two in the Gel,
One in the Smell.

Two in the Flaps,
One in the Traps.

Two in the Tube,
One in the Lube.

Two in the Joy,
One in the Roy.

Two in the Cherry,
One in the Harry.

Two in the Cut,
One in the Butt.

Two in the Eve,
One in the Heave.

Two in the Slot,
One in the Pot.

Two in the Slurp,
One in the Burp.

Two in the Gore,
One in the Whore.

Two in the Bible,
One in the Tribal.

Two in the Clinch,
One in the Pinch.

Two in the Snatch,
One in the Hatch.

Two in the Snapper,
One in the Crapper.

Two in the River,
One in the Shiver.

Two in the Munging,
One in the Plunging.

Two in the Birds,
One in the Turds.

Two in the Funk,
One in the Chunks.

Two in the Sperms,
One in the Germs.

Two in the Kids,
One in the Skids.

Two in the Meadow,
One in the Ghetto.

Two in the Cigar,
One in the Bizarre.

Two in the Tasty,
One in the Hasty.

Two in the Pumper,
One in the Dumper.

Two in the Beaver,
One in the Cleaver.

Two in the Shag,
One in the Wag.

Two in the Hay,
One in the Gay.

Two in the Whack,
One in the Back.

Two in the Dirty,
One in the Hurty.

Two in the Cave,
One in the Slave.

Two in the Chicken,
One in the Sicken.

Two in the Cooter,
One in the Tooter.

Two in the Ho,
One in the Bro.

Two in the Tar,
One in the Star.

Two in the Bled,
One in the Sore and Red.


Two in the Pee,
One in the Glee.


Two in the Chew,
One in the Poo.


Two in the Salt,
One in the Halt!


Two in the Pout,
One in the Doubt.

Two in the Pumpkin,
One in the Blumpkin.

Two in the Bush,
One in the Tush.

Two in the Slit,
One in the Sit.

Two in the Piss,
One in the Fist.

Two in the Yeast,
One in the Feast.

Two in the Bean,
One in the Ravine.


Two in the Friend,
One in...


# The End.

# Also Available

## The Shocker Calendar
shockercalendar.com

## The Shocker for Android
### Coming Soon!
shockerapp.com

# About the Author

Chadsworth "Rad Chad" Brody is as mysterious in origin as the shocker itself. We do know that he was born and raised in an Orange County suburb, and that he later attended a California university where he was very active in a fraternity. Currently, he is reputed to either work in sales in Los Angeles, or as a professional gambler and pick up artist in Las Vegas.

CPSIA information can be obtained at www.ICGtesting.com
Printed in the USA
BVOW05s1202171214

379119BV00005B/76/P